true friend

By Melvina Young

Hallmark

GIFT BOOKS

family is the Love you're given.
friendship is the Love you choose.

I'll always love
you
for choosing
me.

you don't have to put on a cape
for me to know you're my hero.

Just being here
is enough.

YOU HAVE SUCH *STRONG* SHOULDERS...

I know I can
stop and lean
for a while
if I need to.

you always come to my pity parties.

Thanks
for being
my
"PLUS ONE."

can you have more than one better half?

Just asking,

since I'm

a Better person

with you

in my life.

caLL me, DROP a NOTE, SEND a text,
OR SEND UP a flare.
WHEN YOU NEED me, I'M THERE,

just like

you're

there

for me.

good heart,
strong spirit,
kind soul,
true friend...

that's
you.

it's not that other people don't get me at all...

it's that YOU

get me

COMPLETELY.

you celebrate my victories.
you cry over my disappointments.
you have my back during challenges.

You are
just the
FRIEND
I need.

NO MATTER HOW LONG AGO we met,
I'LL ALWAYS feel as if
we've BEEN FRIENDS *forever*.

Trust like friends.

Love
like family.

That's what we do.

a *good* friend tells you when you have spinach in your teeth.

a *great* friend tells you that ordering the sundae instead is the *best* way to avoid getting spinach in your teeth.

know how i know
we're friends for Life?

I can tell you
anything...
and you still
like me anyway.

even when i don't have all the words,
you know what i want to say.

That's how much
you get me.

the economy might be shaky,
but our friendship is not.

THANKS
FOR BEING SO
staBLe.

YOU ARE THE BRINGER
of *good things* to my Life.

IN THIS FRIENDSHIP,
the Love we've *given*
IS THE LOVE
we've *gained*.

when i think of you, i smile.

You
make me
look happy
a lot.

time-sharer

straight-talker

mind-reader

good-thought-sender

support-lender

hug-giver

memory-collector

spirit-lifter

Life-saver.

tHere are over six billion people
in this world...

and

not one

of them

is as

special as

you.

recipe for a great friend:

one part Listener

one part talker

all parts heart

Even if I go

mess

things

up,

you are

always here

when I

get back.

WHEN my LIfe gets totaLLy puzzLIng...

you
help me
get the
pieces
back
into place.

WHY DO I PUT UP WITH YOU?

Oh,
yeah...
'cause
you
put up
with
me.

when I need your support,
I never hesitate to ask...

Because you've

never hesitated

to be there.

you know
that one exercise
where one person
falls back and trusts
the other person
to catch them?

I feel like
we've done that
for each other
a million times.

IS THERE ANYTHING
YOU DON'T KNOW ABOUT ME?

if there is, I bet
I don't
know it
either.

WHEN THERE ARE TIMES THAT ARE JUST
TOO HARD TO DO ALONE...YOU DON'T HAVE TO.

Because I'll be here for you

WHEN
WHER ever.

I was thinking, "there just are no words to describe what you mean to me."

Then I thought,
yes, there is...it's
"everything."

OUR *friendship* is a Lifelong bargain between us...

AND
WE'RE EACH
HOLDING UP
OUR END.

things i can count on:

1. Sun coming up in the morning.

2. Sky darkening at night.

3.

your

friendship

brightening

my life.

that *one look* from you
and i totally lose it.

So much
of what we
"taLk" about
doesn't even
have to be
said aloud.

we're not just friends,
we're *best* friends.

We're
OVERACHIEVERS
like that.

between you and me,
there's no
"TMI."

There's

just

" **I**."

you are the *sunbeam*

that always

manages to

BREAK THROUGH

on my

rainy days.

you've got so much *positive energy*
you could charge my cell phone.

Thanks
for
keeping me
UP
AND
RUNNING.

the more i know you,

the more you

supersize

our good times together.

you ignore my faults
(not that i have any).

But if I did,

I know you'd

ignore them.

over time, our friendship

has really grown up.

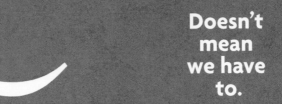

Doesn't mean we have to.

remember that time I...

and then you...

when we lean on each other

we

both

stand

taLL.

HAVING me as a friend means
you'll *NEVER BE ALONE.*

Okay,

you can be alone

in the bathroom.

But otherwise,

I'm right here.

you've written me
so many reality checks...

I'LL

owe

you

for

Life.

what I wish for you, friend:
more *happiness* than you can hold,

more *hugs* than you can return,

more *Laughter* than you can make,

and more *good things* than you

can even imagine.

You DESERVE it.

It's great that you and I
don't have to be *exactly* alike

for you
to be
exactly
the friend
i need.

I always want *good things* for you.

Even things
that could
make me
just
a tiny bit
jealous.

you meet Life
with open arms and the strength
to embrace whatever comes.
you face each day
with the wit and wisdom
to carry you through.

I

aDmiRe

that

about

you.

a *sense of belonging* to something good—
that's what your friendship gives me.

You make the

"good Life"

a little bit good-er.

I can't count *how many times* you've been there for me...

BUT I'LL
NEVER
FORGET
*a SINGLE
ONE.*

IF YOU HAVE ENJOYED THIS BOOK
OR IT HAS TOUCHED YOUR LIFE IN SOME WAY,
WE WOULD LOVE TO HEAR FROM YOU.

Please send your comments to:
Hallmark Book Feedback
P.O. Box 419034
Mail Drop 215
Kansas City, MO 64141

Or e-mail us at:
booknotes@hallmark.com